That's My Dog

SIBERIAN HUSKIES

by Tammy Gagne

FOCUS READERS

FOCUS READERS

www.focusreaders.com

Focus Readers is distributed by North Star Editions:
sales@northstareditions.com | 888-417-0195

Produced for Focus Readers by Red Line Editorial.

Photographs ©: SVPhilon/iStockphoto, cover, 1; iPics/Shutterstock Images, 4–5; gillmar/Shutterstock Images, 6, 29; Image courtesy of 3D Systems, Inc., 8–9; 8213erika/iStockphoto, 10–11; Eric A. Hegg/University of Washington Libraries/Special Collections/Hegg 2262, 12; cpaulfell/Shutterstock Images, 15; Natalia Fadosova/Shutterstock Images, 16–17; Andrey Kuzmin/Shutterstock Images, 18; Ztranger/iStockphoto, 20; Anurak Pongpatimet/iStockphoto, 22–23; Yuriy Koronovskiy/Shutterstock Images, 24; Scharfsinn/Shutterstock Images, 26

ISBN
978-1-63517-544-8 (hardcover)
978-1-63517-616-2 (paperback)
978-1-63517-760-2 (ebook pdf)
978-1-63517-688-9 (hosted ebook)

Library of Congress Control Number: 2017948135

Printed in the United States of America
Mankato, MN
November, 2017

About the Author

Tammy Gagne has written more than 150 books for adults and children. She resides in northern New England with her husband and son. One of her favorite pastimes is visiting schools to talk to kids about the writing process.

TABLE OF CONTENTS

CHAPTER 1

MEET THE SIBERIAN HUSKY

Huskies **descended** from wolves. But unlike wolves, huskies like to spend time with people. Huskies are even friendly with kids. They also get along well with other dogs.

Huskies are sometimes mistaken for wolves.

When pulling a sled, huskies work together in a team.

Huskies are smart dogs. This makes them easy to train. But they need attention. A husky might chew up its owners' belongings if the dog is left alone too long.

Siberian huskies are often used to pull dogsleds. The **breed** is known for their strong bodies. The dogs have heavy coats of thick fur. These features make huskies ideal for work in cold **climates**.

FUN FACT

Huskies are known for being clean. Unlike many other breeds, huskies do not develop odors if they are not bathed frequently.

THAT'S AMAZING!

3D-PRINTED LEGS

A Siberian husky named Derby was born with very short legs. He had a hard time walking without falling. Tara Anderson met Derby at a dog rescue. She decided to help him walk again.

At first she tried using a set of wheels. But they did not work well. Then she got an idea. Anderson works for a company that specializes in three-dimensional (3D) printing. She and her coworkers measured Derby's body by scanning it. Then they 3D-printed a pair of legs for him. Derby soon learned how to walk on his new legs.

Derby's 3D-printed legs even allow him to run!

CHAPTER 2

A WORK HISTORY

The first Siberian huskies came from Siberia. This is an area of Russia that can be very cold. The Chukchi people bred huskies. They used huskies to pull heavy sleds across long distances.

Traveling with a team of sled dogs is also called mushing.

Teams of sled dogs could move Alaskan gold more easily.

Some early huskies were also used as watchdogs. They protected their owners. Other huskies were used to **herd** reindeer.

People brought huskies to Alaska during the late 1800s and early

1900s. At this time, Alaska was not yet a state. Gold was found in the region. Many people traveled there to search for more gold. These people were called **prospectors**. They hoped the gold would make them rich. They used huskies' sled-pulling skills to help them get around Alaska.

FUN FACT

A Siberian husky sled dog team won the All Alaska Sweepstakes Race in 1910.

Soon people brought Siberian huskies farther south. In time, the breed became popular in the United States. Many people had huskies as pets. The US climate isn't as cold as that of Siberia. But the husky breed is still built to withstand snow and cold weather.

FUN FACT

A Siberian husky named Balto led an important mission in 1925. He led a team that brought medicine to people in the remote city of Nome, Alaska.

Many people might have died if not for Balto's mission.

CHAPTER 3

LOOK AT THOSE EYES!

Siberian huskies come in many colors. Some huskies are a solid color. Others are black and white or gray and white. They can even be red and white.

A husky's thick coat keeps it warm in the snow.

A husky's ears are pointed.

Most Siberian huskies have white markings on their faces. These markings are called **masks**.

The Siberian husky is one of the few dog breeds that can have blue eyes. Huskies can also have brown eyes. Some huskies' eyes are a combination of these colors. These dogs are called parti-eyed. Other huskies even have one blue and one brown eye. They are called bi-eyed dogs.

FUN FACT

The Siberian husky is a spitz. This dog type has pointy ears and a bushy tail that curls over the dog's back.

A female husky usually has a litter of four to six puppies at a time.

Husky puppies usually reach their adult height at one year old. It might take another year to reach their full weight. Male huskies stand 21 to 24 inches (53 to 61 cm) tall. They usually weigh 45 to 60 pounds (20 to 27 kg). Females are often a bit smaller than males. They stand 20 to 22 inches (51 to 56 cm) tall. Female huskies usually weigh 35 to 50 pounds (16 to 23 kg).

FUN FACT

The Siberian husky's large paws work like snowshoes. Hair between the toes keeps the dog's feet warm when walking in snow.

CHAPTER 4

A BIG JOB

Siberian huskies need lots of attention. They love spending time with their owners. They enjoy playing outside, too. Huskies can stay outside even when the weather is cooler in the winter.

Husky puppies are small enough to hold, but they quickly grow too big.

Huskies shed heavily in the spring.

Owners must remember that their pets have heavy coats. When warmer weather arrives, huskies need shade if they are going to play outdoors. When indoors, they need air conditioning to stay cool.

A Siberian husky's thick coat needs regular brushing. It is important to brush a husky's coat at least once each week. Most huskies **shed** heavily once every year. This process is called **coat blowing**.

FUN FACT

It can take up to six weeks for a husky to blow its coat.

Walking is a great way for a husky to get exercise.

Owners can cut down on shedding at this time by brushing their husky frequently.

One of the most important parts of caring for a husky is keeping it on a leash in public. This breed can be talented at escaping. Many huskies easily slip their heads out of their collars. They are also known for climbing over fences or crawling under them. But with training, Siberian huskies make great pets.

FUN FACT

Huskies that live in colder climates shed less than those in warmer ones.

FOCUS ON

SIBERIAN HUSKIES

Write your answers on a separate piece of paper.

1. Write a sentence that describes the key ideas from Chapter 2.
2. If you were to own a Siberian husky as a pet, would you like it to be a sled dog? Why or why not?
3. How often should an owner brush a husky?
   - **A.** once a week
   - **B.** once a month
   - **C.** once a year
4. What might happen if an owner left a husky outside too long in the summer?
   - **A.** The dog's eyes would change color.
   - **B.** The dog would not shed as much.
   - **C.** The dog would get too hot.

5. What does **watchdogs** mean in this book?

Some early huskies were also used as ***watchdogs****. They protected their owners.*

- **A.** dogs that guard homes
- **B.** dogs that like to nap
- **C.** dogs that can run fast

6. What does **collars** mean in this book?

This breed can be talented at escaping. Many huskies easily slip their heads out of their ***collars****.*

- **A.** the top parts of people's shirts
- **B.** the front parts of dogsleds
- **C.** bands worn around dogs' necks

Answer key on page 32.

GLOSSARY

breed
A group of animals that share the same looks and features.

climates
The average weather conditions of particular places or regions.

coat blowing
A period of intense shedding that occurs once or twice each year.

descended
Came from a particular family or ancestor.

herd
To keep or look after livestock.

masks
Markings on animals' faces.

prospectors
People who search for valuable materials such as gold.

shed
To release dead hair.

TO LEARN MORE

BOOKS

Gagne, Tammy. *Huskies, Mastiffs, and Other Working Dogs*. Mankato, MN: Capstone Press, 2017.

Johnson, Jinny. *Siberian Husky*. Mankato, MN: Smart Apple Media, 2015.

Newman, Aline Alexander, and Gary Weitzman. *How to Speak Dog: A Guide to Decoding Dog Language*. Washington, DC: National Geographic, 2013.

NOTE TO EDUCATORS

Visit **www.focusreaders.com** to find lesson plans, activities, links, and other resources related to this title.

INDEX

Answer Key: 1. Answers will vary; **2.** Answers will vary; **3.** A; **4.** C; **5.** A; **6.** C